THRIFT

BY

ORISON SWETT MARDEN
Author of "Character," "Cheerfulness," etc.

Sun Books / Sun Publishing

First Sun Books Printing...1997

Sun Books
are Published by
Sun Publishing Company
P.O. Box 5588 Santa Fe,
NM 87502-5588 U.S.A.

ISBN: 0-89540-393-5

TABLE OF CONTENTS

PAGE

I. Thrift, the Foundation of All Greatness 1

II. A Safeguard for the Future 6

III. The Man We Trust 14

IV. Can You Finance Yourself? 21

V. The Art of Saving is the Art of Wise Spending 33

VI. Sailing Under False Colors 41

VII. The Ruin of Rivalry 49

VIII. "A Home of My Own" 57

IX. "He That Soweth Sparingly Shall Reap Sparingly" 68

X. Spendthrifts of Time and Energy . . 78

XI. The Bank-Book Habit 85

TO MY GOOD FRIEND

JAMES A. NEAL

ANDREW CARNEGIE

THRIFT

I

THRIFT, THE FOUNDATION OF ALL GREATNESS

THE term thrift is not only properly applied to money matters, but to everything in life—the wise use of one's time, the wise use of one's ability, one's energy, and this means prudent living, careful habits of life. Thrift is scientific management of one's self, one's time, one's affairs, one's money, the wisest possible expenditure of what we have of all of life's resources.

Thrift is the friend of man, a civilization builder. The practice of thrift gives an upward tendency to the life of the individual, and to the life of the nation; it sustains and preserves the highest welfare of the race.

Lord Rosebery, writing on Thrift,—said that all great empires that were meant to abide, were thrifty.

"Take the Roman Empire, which in some respects, as a centered empire, was the greatest in history," he said; "it lay like an iron clamp upon the face of the world: it was founded on thrift, and when it ceased to be thrifty it degenerated and came to an end. Take the case of Prussia. It began with a little, narrow, strip of sand in the North of Europe—'all sting,' as some one said, from its shape and the fact that its inhabitants were almost all armed men—and it was nurtured by the thrift of Frederick the Great's father, who prepared a vast treasure and a vast army by an economy which we should call sordid, but which was the weapon by which the greatness of Prussia was founded, and from which the present German Empire has risen. Take the case of France. In my humble belief France is in reality the most frugal of all nations. I am not sure that the French always put their money into the savings banks, and, therefore, they do not figure so well in the proportion of depositors to the nation as some others may do; but, after the disastrous year of 1870, when France was crushed for a time by a foreign enemy and by a money imposition which it seemed almost impossible that any nation could pay, what happened? The stockings of the French peasantry, in which they had kept their savings for years, were emptied into the chest of the State, and that huge indemnity and that war expense was paid off in a time incredibly short. The other two nations that I have spoken of were made by their thrift, but France was saved by her thrift."

France, saved by her thrift to save democracy! Now it is our opportunity and privilege, by her great example to establish, both in the home and in the nation, such thrift that we can bountifully extend our aid to this brave ally, let us, every one of us, gladly do our part to sustain her at this critical period, so that she may be preserved and her future assured as one of the great nations of the world! What is saved now, is saved for that country and for our own, for the war, for the victory of civilization.

Thrift is not only one of the foundation-stones of a fortune, but also the foundation of much that is excellent in character. It improves the quality of the individual. The exercise of thrift has a very healthful reaction upon all the other faculties. Thrift is an indication of superiority in many ways. The habit of thrift denotes self-control. It is a proof that a man is not a hopeless victim of his appetites, his weaknesses, but that he is master of himself as well as of his finances.

We know that a thrifty man will not be slovenly, that he will have a certain amount of system and order; that he will be energetic and industrious, and that he is much more likely to be honest than the thriftless man.

Thrift is an educator. A thrifty man thinks and plans. He must have a programme. He must have a certain amount of independence.

If you have cultivated thrift it means that you have demonstrated your ability to control your desires; that you have begun to master yourself, that you are developing some of the grandest human qualities—self-reliance, independence, prudence, foresight; that you are developing your resourcefulness, inventiveness. In other words, it indicates that you have a purpose in life, that you are a man.

"Thrift does not require superior courage, nor superior intellect, nor any superhuman virtue," says a writer on this subject. "It merely requires common-sense and the power of resisting selfish enjoyments. In fact, thrift is merely common-sense in every-day working action. It needs no fervent resolution, but only a little patient self-denial. *Begin* is its device! The more the habit of thrift is practiced the easier it becomes and the sooner it compensates the self-denier for the sacrifice which it has imposed."

II

A SAFEGUARD FOR THE FUTURE

HERBERT SPENCER said that the chief difference between the savage and the civilized man is in the former's lack of foresight. Notwithstanding the hardships of the primitive life, the savage but slowly learns to practice self-denial in order to provide for remote contingencies. Given ample provision for to-day he has no anxiety over the uncertainty of to-morrow.

It is every one's duty to give some thought to the future, to keep in mind a *comfortable* old age.

The possession of money in reserve gives an independence which is an encouragement to effort, just as it is a safeguard for the future. It enables a man to work with more confidence, to look up and not down, to rise superior to his surroundings and not be dragged down by them.

When we get a little money ahead it arouses enthusiasm to add to it. It is a perpetual suggestion to save. It makes it a little easier to say "No" when inclined to spend foolishly or for things which are really not worth while. His small savings have kept many a young man from falling into temptations which might have crippled or ruined him.

The little difference between what we earn and what we spend is capital, an asset. Savings suggest to a young couple just establishing a home wonderful possibilities. Money saved means a better home, more comforts. It means a little more reading matter and better books and periodicals. It means a possible college course later on for the children, and protection for our old age. It means an opportunity to help others—perhaps our country—when the call comes. It means sound sleep, less worry and less anxiety about the future; it means exemption from the horror of horrors, fear of coming to want, anxiety lest those dear to us may suffer for lack of the comforts of life. It may mean the difference between a skillful surgeon or physician and a bungler, in a case of life or death, when sickness enters our home.

I know a very brilliant young man who earned a great deal of money, but who felt such confidence in his continued ability to earn that he recklessly spent every cent as he went along. Suddenly his young wife was taken seriously ill, and in order to save her life he was obliged to get a noted surgeon to perform a very delicate and dangerous operation. As the surgeon would not operate until he was assured of his fee, the young man was compelled to borrow the necessary sum, which was very large. His wife's life was saved, but her continued illness and the illness of their small children, together with the wear and anxiety, so injured the young man's health, that his earning capacity was impaired for many years. In fact, his career was very seriously handicapped, and he and his family suffered many privations for lack of ready money to tide them over their difficulties. This young man could easily have saved a thousand dollars in a single year before his wife's illness, but he did not think it necessary, and believed in living up to his income as he went along. He took no thought for the future.

We never can tell when illness, or accident, may impair our earning capacity, or when some unforeseen emergency may make an unexpected call upon us. Tens of thousands of mothers and children have endured all sorts of hardships because the father never laid up any money for an emergency, and when it came there was no savings-bank balance to help them over their time of stress.

In an address on "The Greater Thrift" delivered before the National Education Association in New York, S. W. Strauss, President of the American Society for Thrift, made this statement: "The records of the Surrogates' Courts show that out of one hundred men who die, three leave estates of $10,000. Fifteen others leave estates from two to ten thousand dollars. Eighty-two of every hundred leave no income-producing estates at all. Thus, out of every one hundred widows, only eighteen are left in good or comfortable circumstances. Forty-seven others are obliged to go to work and thirty-five are left in absolute want."

"I have little respect for the man who does not put himself in a position both to provide and retain enough material means to support comfortably those who are dependent upon him," says Colonel Roosevelt. "It is every man's sacred duty to invest a certain percentage of his earnings for the protection of those depending upon him. It is not so much a question of whether it is a good business investment; it is a duty, a sacred duty, and he will be cruelly unjust to those he loves if he allows them to take a risk which he, personally, conscious of strength and power, might be justified himself in taking. Moreover the feeling that those dearest to him are provided for in case of his death, or any misfortune which may come to his business from changed conditions or bad management, must give an immense satisfaction to any man."

I know of nothing else which quite takes the place of a little ready money in case of need; something which will be a buffer between us and the rough knocks of the world. No one who can possibly afford it should be without such a buffer.

Unless you are thrifty with your money, with your time, you are not success organized. Of course, there are many fine, lovable people, often geniuses in some direction, who are totally lacking in the sense of money values, and spend money,—when they have it—recklessly.

But just in so far as they fail to make wise provisions for the morrow, are they ill-balanced, and on a par with the primitive savage.

People who chafe under little privations, who cannot bear to deny themselves anything, but who are led by their impulses, who are not willing at times to forego a little temporary pleasure that they may lay aside something for the future, will always be handicapped.

How many splendid opportunities we lose in life for the lack of a little ready money, just because we spent everything as we went along and laid aside nothing! Get a little money ahead, something in the bank, put your savings in an insurance policy or some other good, solid investment,—there is nothing safer or better to-day than Liberty Bonds—to give protection in case of emergency.

I know a very brilliant man with remarkable earning capacity, but no saving ability, who lost an opportunity to buy the original Bell telephone stock, before it was watered, for fifty cents a share. The opportunity came to him, but he had to say "No," because he had spent everything as he went along. He has earned a great deal of money, but is always "hard up," and is constantly borrowing from his friends.

The power of ready money is usually not half appreciated by young men and young women. This is a land of opportunity, and good chances are constantly coming to those who have the ready cash. How often we hear people plead as an excuse for not seizing a rare opportunity for investment, that they had no ready money. There are always plenty of opportunities, if one only has a little reserve laid by.

Every young person should have foresight and shrewdness enough to protect some of his savings, not only to keep him from any possible want in case of sickness, death, or emergency, but also to enable him to get a start again, provided he should meet unexpected losses. Without such a reserve he may be handicapped for years, especially if he has a family depending upon him.

A relatively small amount of ready money has saved many a fortune in a case of panic or emergency. There are times in most people's lives when they must have ready money, and must have it immediately. Perhaps a thousand dollars in cash would make all the difference between success and failure, and because they do not have the thousand they fail and often become victims of despair.

It is very difficult to get a hold again after you have once lost your grip, especially in middle life! Many employers look with distrust on gray hairs seeking a livelihood. They think there is something wrong somewhere when a man of years has nothing between himself and want.

To realize that the best years, the most productive years of one's life have gone by, leaving no protection for old age, is certainly disheartening.

The world looks very different to the man who has something laid aside for an emergency, for sickness, or for the comforts of old age, to what it does to the man who has nothing ahead. The man who saves is insuring against all sorts of misfortunes which may come to himself and those dear to him in the future. He is building around his home a wall of protection from insults, from unkind treatment, from cold selfishness of others.

III

THE MAN WE TRUST

Before people will back a man with capital, before bankers will loan him money or jobbers give him credit, they want to know what sort of a man he is. They will inquire into his habits, for they know these will indicate his character.

"Is he stable in his character? Does he save his money? Has he formed habits of thrift? Can his word be relied upon? Has he good business ability? Is he industrious and sober?" These are the first questions which a banker will ask in investigating a man who has applied for a loan. The same thing is true of the jobbers of whom he asks credit. Business men know that it is pretty safe to trust a young man who has developed the habit of thrift, who is careful of his time, his health, his savings.

The quality which increases the confidence of others in a young man and adds tremendously to his credit is the reputation of stability, of soundness of judgment in business matters. If a man is known to be careless in money matters; if he is not prompt in his payments; if he is inclined to gamble, and does not have much faculty for holding on to his money, he will have very hard work to get credit or to start in business for himself.

Every sound business man knows that if a man cannot control himself; if he cannot resist the temptation to spend every bit of his income, perhaps more, in unnecessary ways, in foolish indulgences, he cannot be trusted with money. The man who cannot hold on to his money, who spends it rashly, no matter how honest he may be is always an easy dupe of others, who take advantage of him and his gullibility.

Nothing will do more to help a young man to get credit and gain for him the assistance of successful people than the reputation of having the saving habit,—of having something laid by, whether in government bonds, or in a life insurance policy, or in some other investment. Such thrift gives him standing.

A prominent business man says: "Give me

the youth who saves to make the man worth while."

Every employer knows that the employee who always manages to save something out of his salary, has other sterling qualities, because thrift belongs to a large and most excellent family.

The man who has a fair salary, but who does not lay up anything, is looked upon with suspicion, either as to his ability or his habits. Level-headed business men always think well of young men who, no matter how little they earn, manage somehow to save part of it. Our savings are a power, not only for the money they represent, but because they are evidences of self-denial, good judgment, thrift.

The very fact that a young man has the foresight to look ahead, to provide for the future, for others, or against accident, indicates that he possesses fine qualities of mind and heart, and that he is a good citizen and neighbor. People have confidence in him. The reputation of being provident and a good citizen means more credit, more capital, more influence.

Yet there are young people so foolish as to

boast of spending everything they can get, and that they are always in debt. And there are thousands of young men receiving good salaries—some of them very large—who never think of laying up a dollar. They never see anything in their salaries but a "good time," and they never develop the habit of thrift. You ask them how they are doing, and they will say: "Oh, just getting along," "just making a living," "just holding my own."

Just making a bare living is not getting on, and it is not sufficient recommendation.

Bacon says that a man who would live well within his income ought not to expend more than one-half, and should save the rest.

I knew a young man who had received a good salary for many years, and who had never saved a dollar, but who always intended to save. Every year he thought he was going to save several hundred dollars at least out of his salary; but at the end of the year he always found that all of his money was gone.

One day someone asked him what he had done with his salary the past year. It set him thinking. Up to that time he had never kept an account of his expenditures; but he sat down and began to figure up his necessary expenses, and found that they were not equal to one-quarter of his salary. Three-fourths of all he earned had gone for amusement and trifles. He resolved then and there to save half of his salary, and at once opened an account in a savings bank and deposited what he had. He did not make the fatal mistake, which many make, of waiting until he had a large amount to deposit.

In a short time this young man was not only surprised to see how easy it was to save when he had a strong motive but he was also surprised at the pleasure he had in saving, in watching his account grow, and in planning for a home of his own and to go into business for himself. At the end of the first year he had a splendid balance in the bank, and yet he could not see that he had missed any pleasure which would have been of real benefit to him. He had cut off habits which were injurious to him, and which only made him hate himself for indulgence in them, and with his increasing self-respect, he had formed the habit of reading and self-improvement. Everybody who knew him noticed the great change in his appearance, and it was not long before he was offered a partnership in a good business.

"I have often been asked," says a prominent business man, "to define the true secret of success. *It is thrift in all its phases,* and especially thrift as applied to saving. Saving is the first great principle of success. It creates independence, it gives a young man standing, fills him with vigor, it stimulates him with the proper energy; in fact, it brings to him the best part of any success—happiness and contentment."

No matter how well you are doing in your business or how large a salary you are getting, do not spend it all as you go, for your most effective years do not last very long, and if you spend everything you earn in those years how can you expect comfort and ease in old age?

Perhaps the great majority of people do their best work and earn their largest amount of money during fifteen or twenty years. Your future comfort and happiness depend on the surplus of your most productive years. Do not risk too much on your prospects for the future. Save to-day. Take no chances with your home. Make a sure thing of it. Never mind the little sacrifices you make to-day. You can afford them for the sake of to-morrow.

Make a cast-iron rule to lay aside a certain percentage of your earnings every year. No matter how small it may be, or if you have to go without a great many things that you think you need, put a certain percentage of your earnings where it will be absolutely safe. Thrift Stamps are a safe foundation on which to build your happiness and welfare. You will find there is a great satisfaction not only in seeing your little savings grow, but in knowing that such investment on your part, small as it may be, is helping your country to bear its burdens at a critical time.

The great majority of people are incapable of doing large things—it would be impossible for them to raise any considerable amount of money at once—but the great mass of people can put aside a certain amount from their incomes or salaries and thus provide for the future.

IV

CAN YOU FINANCE YOURSELF?

A MOST essential thing for every one to know is how to finance oneself—how to earn and use money. It does not matter how much you know or how educated you are, if you cannot finance or support yourself there is something wrong in your education and your training; you are deficient, no matter how talented in other respects.

One of the most pathetic phases of American life is that so many people are leading unhappy, wretched lives because in their youth they were not taught how to finance themselves, or to earn their own living. How many thousands of our young women have been placed at the mercy of chance, because they lacked training in this respect! From childhood the idea was instilled in them that when they "grew up" they were expected to marry. Whether they ought to marry or not, regardless of any special talent they might have for business or for a profession, regardless of whether they had a special mission for the world, they were supposed to look out for a husband. It was not considered necessary or desirable that the daughter should have any special training to fit her for a business or independent career. Reared as a dependent creature the girl of the past was a sort of clinging vine, brought up to think that someone would take care of her, so far as her living was concerned; that her father would look out for her until she married, and then her husband would do the rest.

Think of the position of a self-respecting girl, with perhaps no desire or opportunity to marry, when she reached maturity and felt that her parents expected her to relieve them of her support yet realized she was perfectly helpless to do so! She had never been taught to earn her living, what was she to do under such circumstances? She found herself growing older and older, and did not want to marry, yet there seemed nothing else for her to do.

To those with modern ideas there are plenty of useful careers besides that of matrimony open to the girl of to-day. The war is presenting new and wonderful opportunities to women, and they are developing marvelous resourcefulness, inventiveness, vast ability which they never before dreamed they possessed. This new outlook for woman, with her new independence, her new self-reliance, will give her a chance which she never before had. The educated girl of to-day knows she is under no obligation whatever to marry unless there is a loud, unmistakable call in her nature, and of this she should be the judge.

The fact that they were totally untrained to earn their living; or at best not sufficiently trained to make it possible for them to earn more than a bare subsistence, has had a blighting effect on many promising young lives.

There are many women to-day who are perfectly miserable because their whole natures have revolted at the idea of marriage, but they were practically obliged to leave home, and they believed there was no other door open for them. They had never been trained in any money-making profession that would assure them independence. Is it surprising that such women prove inefficient, thriftless wives, and when widowed are incapable of self-support?

To my mind it is not only cruel, but really a crime, to force a girl, when she is hopelessly inefficient, out into the world to earn her living, or to marry a man who is totally unsuited to make her happy or to be the father of her children, the head of a family.

Parents, make your girl self-reliant, so that men will know that she is not dependent upon any one of them for support, that she is perfectly capable not only of making a living, but of making a career of distinction, because of her education and expert training in some particular line. Most girls are just as proud of making a reputation along the lines of their ability as are the men, and they should have the same chance that their brothers have to develop their business possibilities.

Many a cultured girl has been thrown suddenly on her own resources by the failure or the death of her father, and has found herself wholly incapable of administering his affairs or of earning a living. Many women, when their husbands die suddenly, are left with business responsibilities, which they are utterly unfit to assume. They are at the mercy of designing lawyers or dishonest business men, who well know that they are mere babies in their hands, when it comes to important business transactions.

Business talent is as rare as a talent for mathematics. We find boys and girls turned out of school and college full of theories, and all sorts of knowledge or smatterings of knowledge, but without the ability to protect themselves from human thieves who are trying to get something for nothing. No girl or boy should be allowed to graduate, especially from any of the higher institutions, without being well grounded in practical business methods. Parents who send their children out in life without seeing that they are well versed in ordinary business principles do them incalculable injustice.

Thousands of girls are sent out into the world with what is called finished educations, who cannot even give a proper receipt for money, to say nothing of drawing a promissory note, a draft or a bill, or understanding the significance and importance of business contracts. One such woman presented a check for payment to the paying teller of her bank.

He passed it back to her with the request that she be kind enough to indorse it. The lady wrote on the back of the check, "I have done business with this bank for many years, and I believe it to be all right. Mrs. James B. Brown."

If every child in America had a thorough business training, tens of thousands of promoters, longheaded, cunning schemers, who have thriven on the people's ignorance, would be out of an occupation.

Since, as we have seen in a preceding chapter, only eighteen out of every one hundred widows are left independent, forty-seven being obliged to go to work, and the remaining thirty-five being left in absolute want, it is clear that every woman, married or single, should know how to support and finance herself. The necessity for this is made more apparent than ever at this critical period of the world's history, when the male element of the family is being called from the home. It is as imperative to train the girl to be self-supporting as it is to train the boy.

What pitiable cases we often see of young wives, sincere and honest, but who had practically no training in financing themselves or in the handling of money previous to their marriage, who innocently develop extravagant habits in dress, and run in debt for luxuries! How often we find these young women with moderately salaried husbands ordering expensive dishes in restaurants, riding in taxicabs, doing all sorts of things which are not at all in keeping with their husbands' small incomes!

Not long ago a married woman told me that it had never occurred to her, during the years when her father paid all her bills with checks, that, when she got a home of her own and her income was limited, if she paid one hundred dollars for a dress, she could not afford to buy a fifty dollar hat, as she had been accustomed to do before marriage. She said she had suffered terribly in readjusting herself to her husband's limited income, because of her lack of early training in the use and handling of money. She had been reared with the idea that whenever she wanted anything, her father would pay for it. It was several years before she could seem to figure out the proper proportion for her personal expenditures. She said she had never before realized that if she spent her money for one thing, she could not have it for something else.

The wise expenditure of money incurring thrifty habits of living is a matter in which every girl should be well trained before she leaves home. I know fathers who seem to think that they save money by not allowing their daughters to handle it. But if a sensible girl has learned the value of each dollar, she will be very much more careful as to how she spends it.

Most girls are not given an opportunity to handle money until they are mature. Hence, many never learn its real value or how to spend it to the best advantage. They are undeveloped in the ways of thrift. During her school days, the father not only pays for the daughter's clothing, but the mother usually decides of what the clothing shall consist. In other words, instead of giving the daughter an allowance while she is in school, or not in a position to earn anything to speak of, and teaching her how to use her judgment and cultivate her taste in the selection of whatever she wears, thus developing her self-reliance,

From the drawing by Pierre Morand made November 12, 1842, in the possession of Colonel John Jacob Astor.

JOHN JACOB ASTOR.

and making her as self-dependent as possible, the average girl is brought up to lean upon her parents in all such things, and not being accustomed to handle money of her own, or to keep accounts, she often goes to her own home with very little practical sense in money matters. Thousands of girls marry in this weak and helpless condition, and a great deal of discord results in the home, oftentimes wrecking it. How can a girl who has had practically no training in the handling of money, know its value,—all at once become a wise financier when she is married?

When a girl who has been brought up in a very strict home, who has perhaps been over-chaperoned, and over-protected, feels her new-found freedom, her new sense of liberty from restraint, she is naturally led into extravagant expenditures, and is often encouraged by an affectionate indulgent husband, who is anxious to do everything he can to please her.

I know of a pitiable case of this kind where the wife of a young college professor ran up accounts in department stores, at livery stables, even at florists, without realizing what she was doing. Her new-found liberty, away from the restraints of an exacting, penurious father, meant license to this young wife, and she did not know how careful she would need to be in the spending of her husband's small salary of two thousand dollars. She did not stop to consider that her father would no longer send checks for her purchases, and that two thousand dollars a year did not admit of many theater or opera tickets. Before she knew it, she had run up large accounts and not only embarrassed her husband for several years, but also suffered great humiliation and chagrin herself.

When the bills began to arrive and the young wife awoke to the full realization of her situation, rather than tell her husband, she pawned her jewelry, some of which were her wedding presents. But the husband found that out, and was not only greatly shocked at the condition of things, but was seriously troubled because of his wife's deception, even though not intentional.

The world demands that every individual know how to take care of himself, how to be independent, self-reliant, how to finance himself wisely, how to make the most of his income. There is nothing more important to a human being than to be able not only to earn his own living, but also to know how to use his money to the best possible advantage, for on this depends his power to make himself independent and consequently to do his best work in the world.

One of the first steps in financing yourself properly is to keep a personal cash account. This is one of the best educators and teachers of economy and system. If the habit is formed when you are young in years it will never be broken. It will mean a competence in later life when otherwise there may be none.

Very few young women and girls use business methods in the handling of their money. Now, financing yourself is one of the first lessons in the science of success. If you cannot finance yourself in a level-headed, wise way, you certainly cannot wisely manage your own affairs or those of another. Unbusinesslike methods, unwise handling of money will make a bad impression upon your employer, or your husband. If you are not thrifty in your own affairs, if you are not businesslike in managing them, others will take it for granted that you will be inefficient in the handling of their affairs.

However you make your living, whether by the work of your hand or of your brain, in a trade or in a profession, at home or in the shop, whether your income be small or large, you will always be placed at a disadvantage, unless you know how to finance yourself successfully. This is not to be "close," mean or stingy, but to know how to make the most out of your income; not to expend the margin you should save in silly extravagances or to make foolish investments. Let your slogan be, as it is with the nation,—"Economy."

V

THE ART OF SAVING IS THE ART OF WISE SPENDING

"Economy is not meanness, it is managing."

A FEW years ago our newspapers gave space to a certain rich man who made plenty of money from his own work, as well as the work of others, and his very foolish way of spending it. The published report gave the following telegram from Indianapolis:

"Frank Fox, of Pittsburgh, stood in the Hotel English drying his face with a $50 bill. He threw the bill to the floor and then produced from a bundle under his arm a handful of fives and fifties. Throwing them on the bar, he said: 'Bartender, give me a drink, quick, or I will buy this hotel and have you fired.' "

This man's destiny may easily be imagined. His previous history I know nothing about, except that his fortune was amassed by his energy. For him to achieve such wealth a certain amount of economy must have been necessary on his part as well as that of others. But that he never learned the true meaning of thrift is certain, for thrift teaches how to spend as well as how to save. Many people have accumulated money who do not know how to spend it wisely.

Only a little while ago I heard of a young man who was left a large fortune, and who was so intoxicated with the foolish idea that he was going to be a great financier, that he invested right and left in all sorts of securities. He became so entangled in the schemes of wily promoters, who were quick to discover his gullibility, that, before he knew it, he had run through his entire fortune. Yet he really thought he was making money until the crash came. When he failed, it was found that, in the entire list of his securities there was scarcely anything of real value. There was hardly a security in which any level-headed business man would have risked a dollar.

Most young men have an ambition to make money. There is a personal pride in it. It touches their vanity. They think there is something the matter with a young man who cannot make money. The motive is so strong for money-making that they make a strenuous endeavor to get it; but do not make an equal effort to retain it, there being a thousand and one temptations trying to induce them to give it up.

A self-made millionaire tells me that not one out of a hundred of those who make money in New York can keep it. While this may be exaggerated, we all know that comparatively few are able to keep what they make. The inducements to part with money are very alluring to those who are not strongly intrenched in self-control.

A well-known victim of thriftlessness is the amiable, easy-going, large-hearted, liberal man. He is always ready to pay for the lunch, for the dinner, for the drinks. His bump of generosity is so strongly developed, that everything goes as fast as he gets it. He cannot seem to hold on to money.

This type of a man often has the best intentions, fine impulses, yet he absolutely ruins those dependent upon him, as well as himself, by not providing for their future. Almost anyone can get money from him, if he has any, by asking. If he does not happen to have it, he will often borrow it for his friends. I know a man of this sort, who, but for this one defect, would probably have been a very great success. He has many warm friends; everybody who knows him loves him, yet he has not been able to get capital ahead and his family, those really nearest and dearest to him, are the victims of his prodigality. Such a man might well take a lesson from Goldsmith, who wrote:

"I had learned from books to be disinterested and generous before I was taught from experience the necessity of being prudent . . . . Often by being, even with my narrow finances, charitable to excess, I forgot the rules of justice and placed myself in the very situation of the wretch who thanked me for my bounty." And this man, who could refuse no indulgences either to himself or others, admonished his brother to teach his son thrift and economy. "Let his poor wandering uncle's example be placed before his eyes."

Everyone should be taught the value of money and how to spend it wisely. If people do not acquire this knowledge in youth, they seldom later in life do so.

There is no one human faculty neglected more by the common people than prudence. Men reach ahead and make money, but after they get it, most of them seem powerless to keep it. It slips through their fingers, in an incredible manner, in all sorts of foolish ways.

The art of saving is essentially the art of wise spending. Oftentimes what seems like extravagance is the greatest possible economy. There are many families, especially in smaller towns and in the country, who own automobiles but who have no bathtubs in their homes, and consider the latter expensive luxuries.

We would not discourage people from owning automobiles, because they are a precious boon to the American home, bringing relief to the monotonous existence of women and children, and health, variety, and joy to vast multitudes of people heretofore deprived of these blessings; but cleanliness is not only next to godliness, it is godliness, and most of us consider a bathtub an important adjunct to cleanliness. It took civilization many centuries to arrive at the bathtub as a necessity and luxury. Most of us are finding that the daily bath is a wonderful health and efficiency promoter and life prolonger.

The great thing in making expenditures is to spend upward, to invest in oneself. Do not be content to wear silks and diamonds on the body, to ride around in your limousine, and to dress the mind in calico and the character in rags. Let self-improvement, self-culture, a healthy mind, a fine personality be your richest dress. Spend your money and time on things which endure. Spend them in any way that will make you a larger, grander, truer man or woman. There is infinite satisfaction in spending for the higher instead of the lower, in self-investment, in self-improvement.

Invest in the best things. It is spending upward, living upward, dwelling in honesty, in simplicity, living the life that is worth while, the real life, the sincere life, the genuine life, that will give the greatest satisfaction.

There are people who have very small incomes, and yet they spend it in all sorts of foolish ways. They will take their last penny to buy expensive bric-a-brac and articles of dress, which only the well-to-do could afford to have, and then they suffer for the real necessaries of life.

I know a most excellent woman who was brought up in luxury without learning the value of things, and who is now poor. Quite recently she would go to market and buy the greatest variety of eatables for the table, knowing perfectly well that she would be obliged to go without necessary articles of clothing in order to cover the extravagance. She considers it deplorable not to have a great quantity and a great variety of food on the table. This housekeeper, as well as many others who heretofore spent recklessly for foodstuffs and luxuries, are now taking lessons in thrift from our wise Government.

Most people do not take into consideration the tremendous inducements that are all the time at work trying to get their money away from them. Scores of fancied wants are tugging away at the pocketbook all the time, and unless we are well-grounded in the principles of self-control and caution and prudence, unless we develop good judgment, the money will slip away from us.

There are multitudes of people to-day in

the great failure army, in our poorhouses, or being helped by the charitable associations, who would have been fairly independent to-day had they learned the art of wise spending. "A penny saved instead of a penny properly spent is a penny wasted," we are told. "Why not remember the parable of the talents and learn wisdom from it?"

VI

SAILING UNDER FALSE COLORS

MANY people who are honest in their business dealings are dishonest in their social appearances. They wear all sorts of lies, act all sorts of lies, in order to deceive others in regard to their rank in society. In cities we often see houses built with just a thin layer of brown-stone front, while the rest is made of old second-hand bricks—anything to fill in with—the type of architecture that has been called Queen Anne in front and Mary Ann in the back.

We put plate glass in our front windows and display our costly furnishings in the front of the house, but we often find all sorts of cheap, shabby, shoddy things in the rear. Our characters in these days are much like our houses. We put our best selves before the public. We are not genuine through and through.

Keeping up false appearances, living a false life, is most demoralizing. Trying to make people think you are better off than you really are acts as a boomerang which strikes back with a fatal rebound.

A New York woman of high social ambitions not long ago lost her home and all her property in her efforts to introduce her daughters into fashionable society. The family could have lived in comfort on their modest income, had not the mother gone far beyond their means in her eagerness to force her daughters into the society of those who were socially far above them in the matter of wealth. She spent a great deal of money in giving smart entertainments in order to show her girls off to the best advantage. Thousands of dollars were squandered in buying beautiful gowns, hats, laces, and all sorts of expensive finery for them, so that they might shine as brilliantly as other young ladies who had a hundred times their financial means. In an insane attempt to keep up appearances far beyond her income, and to secure, as she hoped, wealthy husbands for her daughters, she became hopelessly entangled in debt, and was forced into bankruptcy, and the daughters, instead of winning the prizes their mother sought, are mortified and chagrined to find themselves now without even a home.

Mothers in ordinary circumstances often make tremendous efforts to marry their daughters to rich men, little realizing that they are thus making their girls dissatisfied with their humble surroundings, and leading them to think their modest home a bore, a place to be shunned as much as possible. They little know that this catering to vanity is what ruins so many girls and makes selfish, discontented, thriftless wives of them.

Trying to put up a good front, to keep up appearances which we cannot afford, has cast a gloom of unhappiness and misery over thousands of homes which but for envy, but for silly false pride, might have been very happy homes. There is more misery and discontent among the many people who occupy boxes and expensive seats at the theater and the opera than among those who cannot afford a seat at all, but stand up in the rear.

I know of women who enjoy life immensely who cannot afford even the cheapest seats at the opera, but they gladly stand, and return home delighted, radiant with happiness, while one often sees other women, in the most expensive boxes, whose faces are the bulletin boards that show their discontent.

Would you not rather go to the theater in ordinary clothes and in a street-car than to be fashionably attired, go in a limousine, and sit in a box and worry all the evening because you could not afford it, and wondered how you were going to pay your bills?

Who can estimate the suffering, the human tragedies that result from this everlasting strain of trying to keep up appearances, of living beyond one's means? There are plenty of people everywhere to-day who do not have enough to eat, and who practice all sorts of pinching economy at home for the sake of keeping up appearances in society.

What tremendous strides we could make in things that really count were the energy expended in straining to keep up appearances spent in improving ourselves, in genuine self-culture, in man building, in woman building!

Why should it require so much courage to live the life we can afford, to be genuine, true,

BENJAMIN FRANKLIN

and never to fear what our neighbors think? Even those who are wealthy will think more of us for this independence.

Many people shorten their lives in overworking, in plodding along without vacations or change, struggling to keep up appearances, to satisfy others' ideas of what they ought to do and ought to have.

I have watched young people who live this sort of a life, and it is a rare thing that any of them turn out well. Their weakness, the tendency for show, grows upon them, and when they once get a taste of what they call the "good things of life," the luxuries, they develop a dissatisfaction for their humble homes. They immediately think they were born out of their sphere; that it is a shame for people with a taste for luxuries to be poor. They never think they should put forth any honest efforts to bring about a more prosperous condition.

The fact is, that extravagant habits are incompatible with the thrift necessary for success in any career. There must be an underlying, clean-cut thrift in the nature, a disposition to make the most of everything, and to make every dollar go as far as possible, and to save just as much as possible without pinching in one's comforts or being mean.

The people who plunge into extravagance to keep pace with families of the rich overlook the fact that behind every honest fortune lies thrift. If we investigate, we will generally find that the antecedents of these rich people worked hard, lived frugally, practiced economy to lay the foundation of the fortune.

Our real wants are very simple. We could supply them all by working a very small part of our time; but it is the things demanded for others' eyes that are so expensive, that cost our life-blood, that sap our energy, that cause the tremendous life strain, the nervous prostration, the paralysis, the premature old age.

Ah! what tyrants others' eyes are! How we wince under their glance! What a rare thing it is to find a person who is large enough and free enough to be really natural.

How many people live and dress and pose and endure all sorts of inconveniences and slavery just to impress their neighbors! Do what they will, they cannot get away from others' eyes. They have costly draperies at their windows while behind them are filth and disorder and broken-down furniture.

Most of us are always posing, acting, never quite ourselves. We cannot get rid of the consciousness that others are looking at us and that we must put up a good front. The suit, the hat must be discarded, not because they are badly worn, but because others will think it strange that we do not change them. It is sad to think that even while the world lies bleeding, such frivolity exists!

Society is demoralized when the people live far beyond their means, when they sail under false colors, many of them cursed by debt, often resorting to methods bordering on criminality in order to keep up the miserable deceit of appearing richer than they are.

"The standard of living among the rich has been raised to an excessive degree, and those who would like to be thought rich try to follow the lead set by the big financiers and mining magnates who are to our day what the Indian nabobs were to the England of George III," says a writer. "People who live beyond their means are tempted to speculate, and the bankruptcy records show the inevitable result.

A course of plain living and high thinking would be good for the morals of society, and good for legitimate trade."

Why not get down to realities by living the simple life, the natural life, by throwing off masks and being what you seem? This constant straining to appear what you are not, this building up a superficial character, keeping up a deceitful appearance, will honeycomb the life with fraud and leave nothing but dissatisfaction behind.

Do not be afraid to decline to do what you cannot afford. Dare to say "No" with emphasis, to be yourself. Be content to let others make fools of themselves, if they will.

VII

THE RUIN OF RIVALRY

NOT long ago I heard a New York business man with a small income say: "I have no idea of taking a back seat when it comes to putting up a good front." He said that his income would not warrant his keeping an automobile, but he was obliged to have one because his neighbors and others had them, and he did not propose to be outdone by them; that he did not want his children humiliated because they could not afford what others had, and so he ran into a debt which has made him a slave for years.

There are thousands of people striving and struggling in the most unnatural way to get along in New York and other large cities, who are desperately unhappy because of the contrast between their condition and that of those whom they envy. I do not believe there is any place in the world where envy plays such a prominent part as in a great city.

So many people seem to think that it is almost a disgrace not to have what other people whom they know have. If others have an automobile, they must have one, whether they can afford it or not. Daughters of men in narrow circumstances think they must have the same beautiful things to wear as their friends have who may be infinitely better able to afford them. I know young people who say they would rather stay at home than go anywhere unless they can dress as others do and go as others go.

A young man who received twenty dollars a week told me that it cost him fifteen dollars one evening to take a young woman to the opera and to supper afterward. Another young fellow, who only earned eight dollars a week, told me that he frequently spent nearly half that amount in taking a young woman to the theater. Because her other friends could do this, he felt he must. Everywhere we see people in ordinary circumstances aping the rich.

Many of us are such slaves to this imitation of others that we have no time for friendships, no time for social life, no time for true enjoyment, for doing the things that are really worth while.

I know a mother who is not very ambitious for herself, and she is not particularly mortified or very greatly inconvenienced personally by her poverty, but she is very much distressed and humiliated on her daughter's account. She grieves that her child cannot have what other girls whom she knows have, that she must ride on the street-car or walk when other girls have maids to attend them, and luxurious automobiles to take them wherever they wish to go.

She says it breaks her heart to think that her attractive daughter has to wear cheap, ordinary clothing, when other girls not half as attractive or deserving dress in the most extravagant manner and wear expensive jewelry, and that there is something cruelly wrong with a society which forces her daughter to work in an office all day, instead of living a life of ease, with servants and money at her command.

This woman has so poisoned her daughter's mind in talking before her in this way, in bringing her up to despise her humble home and surroundings, that the girl does not appreciate anything she has. Like her mother, she is always comparing her limited condition with the luxurious state of others. The mother has filled the girl's head full of nonsense about making a supreme effort to marry money, and in this way help to replenish the depleted family treasury. She tells her that no matter how honest or industrious a young man may be, if he has not money, if he cannot support a wife in luxury, she should have nothing to do with him. In her desperate efforts to marry her daughter to somebody with money, I doubt very much whether she would ask any questions about a wealthy suitor's character.

Instead of being buoyant, cheerful, happy, optimistic, as all youth naturally are, the daughter is cynical, sarcastic about everything, always complaining of her hard lot. She never seems to enjoy anything she has. It is always cheap and dowdy, never looks right or sets right. Her hat is a "cheapjohn thing"; she "hates it."

Happiness is a mental attitude, it is the condition of the mind, not the condition of the pocketbook, and Nature has made it further impossible for happiness to live in complex, complicated, envious conditions.

If you are made of the right kind of metal you will not allow other people to destroy your peace of mind or your happiness. It is an evidence of weakness if you do; it shows that you have a foolish vanity.

Gratification, satisfaction of our selfish cravings, only increases our soul hunger. "Desire is as insatiable as its demands are attended to."

Human beings starve and pinch their lives and stunt their growth by their wrong attitude toward life. They kill every joy and blight their happiness by their own envy, jealousy, and false ambition.

It is not so much our lack of comforts, or of luxuries, as our envy, our selfishness, our false standards that make us unhappy.

Many of us miss the joys that might be ours by keeping our eyes fixed on those of other people. No one can enjoy his own opportunities for happiness while he is envious of another's. We lose a great deal of the joy of living by not cheerfully accepting the small pleasures that come to us every day, instead of longing and wishing for what belongs to others.

Why not take pleasure in our own modest car, and not long for the luxurious "Twin-Six" that some one else owns? Why let the edge be taken off the enjoyment of our own little home watching the palatial residence of our neighbor? Let us try to get satisfaction out of a trolley ride into the country or a sail on a river steamer, and not envy the man who can enjoy the luxury of his own touring car or yacht. Usually you will find he or some one belonging to him has labored hard for these enjoyments.

"Many people envy the possessions of the rich," says Samuel Smiles, "but will not pass through the risks, the fatigues, or the dangers of acquiring them. It is related of the Duke of Dantzig that an old comrade, whom he had not seen for many years, called upon him at his hotel in Paris, and seemed amazed at the luxury of his apartments, the richness of his furniture, and the magnificence of his gardens. The duke, supposing that he saw in his old comrade's face a feeling of jealousy, said to him bluntly, 'You may have all that you see before you, on one condition.' 'What is that?' said his friend. 'It is that you will place yourself twenty paces off, and let me fire at you with a musket a hundred times.' 'I will certainly not accept your offer at that price.' 'Well,' replied the marshal, 'to gain all that you see before you, I have faced more than a thousand gunshots, fired at not more than ten paces off.' "

A girl arrested in New York for vagrancy was asked by a magistrate what caused her to drift into that sort of a life. She said: "I wanted to dress like other girls, and I couldn't."

A New York woman in the ante-bellum days boasted that she spent two hundred thousand dollars a year for dress. She said she had many dresses every year that cost a thousand dollars or more, that her shoes cost her fifty dollars a pair, the leather being all imported and dyed to match each one of her dresses. She justified this extravagance on the ground that it gave employment to a great many people.

This woman perhaps never stopped to think

of the demoralizing influence of her example upon poor girls. How many are tempted into extravagance which they cannot afford, make slaves of themselves or are tempted into immoral living in trying to ape people of her type?

No greater delusion ever crept into a rich woman's head than that wanton extravagance is justified on the ground that it gives employment. Thousands of girls are ruined every year because of the demoralizing influence of just such examples; besides the multitudes that are rendered unhappy because they cannot obtain those things.

No rich person has a right to set an example which will demoralize others. Our rights to extravagance cease when they injure others. No woman has a right to flaunt her riches in the faces of poor girls, who are made miserable by her foolish, extravagant example.

VIII

"A HOME OF MY OWN"

IN the heart of the average young person lies the desire to possess a home of his own. Unfortunately, most people fail to see the obstacles that lie in the way of their achieving this worthy desire. "A home of my own!" Around this cluster many sweet dreams of fireside joys, but we start wrong in our quest.

With small salaries and limited incomes, how often young men spend extravagantly in their courting days! In their youthful ardor they send the object of their devotion expensive bonbons, costly flowers in winter, and other luxuries out of season; and, without regard to expense, hire automobiles for theater and opera when lower-priced vehicles would answer. All of these things keep back the young man who wants to establish a home of his own. He is not starting right. It gives a wrong impression to his future wife. Expensive bonbons and flowers and costly amusements will not make a sensible girl think any more of you, my friend; she will often think less of you, especially if she knows, or even suspects, that you can't afford the outlay. It does not bespeak a level head, good judgment, sound financial wisdom on your part.

I have often heard girls say that they were sorry their men friends spent so much money on them, because they knew that they could not afford it; but they did not like to say this to them. Some years ago I knew a young man, earning a salary of about twelve dollars a week, who would buy expensive roses for a young woman he admired, and go without his lunches in order to save for them. I have known him, when the object of his devotion was traveling, to telegraph to a distant city to a florist to deliver flowers at her hotel! Notwithstanding this foolish expenditure, he failed to make the impression upon the young woman that he thought he would make. She found that he was not well-balanced, and, after he had expended a great deal of money and seriously embarrassed himself financially trying to win her, she refused to marry him.

If he had been more sensible in his courtship he might have been successful, but the young woman knew he could not afford the extravagant things he did and she lost faith in him.

The temptations to spend on every hand are so alluring that it is very difficult for a young man of ordinary self-control to resist them and save his money. It is very easy, especially in a large city, with all its allurements, to spend one's loose change for cigars, for drinks, theater tickets, dinners at expensive restaurants and hotels, and all sorts of indulgences. These are the things that go far to prevent the accumulation of that first thousand dollars which is so important in the foundation for all one's future success and happiness.

If you really want to make your dreams come true you will enter into a compact with yourself to save a certain amount every week out of your salary.

It is a great thing always to have some object in view. No better one could be found than that of helping your country by investing all you can in War Certificates and Thrift Stamps. Forego the luxuries and extravagances of former days and show your patriotism in this way. Thus you may be able to establish not only habits of thrift and economy, but to bring into reality that home you have been visualizing.

A little money in reserve is a great encourager, a perpetual stimulus to ambition. The consciousness that we are getting on in the world, that we are laying the foundation for the home of our dreams, is a tremendous motive which marvelously increases our courage, our ability, our efficiency.

Thrift is the beginning of success. It puts a foundation under your air castle. It builds that "home of my own" to which every healthy, ambitious young fellow looks forward as the culmination of his hopes.

Who can ever estimate what the saving for a home has done for people! This glorious vision has held vast multitudes of men and women to their task, kept them from yielding to a thousand tempting calls bidding for their money.

Learning how to hold on to money without being mean or stingy with it is a great art. Anything which will induce the habit of saving in this extravagant nation is a blessing. The whole tendency is toward a wicked waste of money, shameful extravagance in living and in social life. No matter how small your income, make it above the line of your expenses, and without being penurious keep as far within this boundary-line as possible.

Only recently I heard a young man boasting that he got a big salary, but he had never laid up a cent in his life, and that often at the end of the week he was behind and had to borrow money. Now, think of a young man boasting of this, and yet expecting to get on in the world, to own a home of his own, to stand for something in his community, to be a man of importance among his fellows!

Most people are entirely too confident about their financial safety. They do not expect the emergencies of illness, of accident, of business, of change of location, losses which war brings, for example, and which panics and fires cause. How many thousands of people to-day are eating the bitter fruit of poverty, grinding penury, are homeless, moneyless, who, if they had but put a little money in the savings bank during their productive years would have had a good home, comforts, and contentment!

On every hand we see people going through life with stooping shoulders, drawn features, slaves of a mortgage or other debts which are sapping the life out of them, making them prematurely old, when they should be in the very prime of life. You can always see the mortgage looking out of the ugly wrinkles which it has made in their faces. Had they sought thrift as their companion through life, how different would have been their lot.

Is there anything more pathetic to see than so many men and women who have reached middle life or later with no home or money, nothing saved for a rainy day, not only without prospects, but many of them without occupations? Parents are often to blame for much of this unfortunate condition, because they did not early inculcate into their children the principles of economy, did not establish in their early careers the habit of thrift.

When you are fifty or more, my young friend, the dollar will look very different to you than it does now, when the years are few, the future full of promise, and you feel so confident of great achievements. As you approach middle life your money possessions will take on new values.

A man cannot respect himself when he is letting slip through his fingers the dollars which he knows ought to be saved. Oh, the sorrow, the suffering inflicted, in tens of thousands of hearts, by men who realize too late that they have lost or squandered money enough to have provided a home or started them in business, to have given them independence, to have provided for their old age!

On every hand, we see people who have never been able to get ahead in the world simply because they were not willing to make early sacrifices, or to bear hardships or privations in order to make good investments for the future. They could not restrain their desires, they must have a good time, they must buy what they wanted, even if they had to run into debt for it.

It would be impossible to estimate the tremendous benefit which savings banks and insurance companies have conferred upon mankind. In tens of thousands of very humble homes we find the light of hope and cheer, a sense of security because there are insurance policies there. The history of many a life insurance policy, how it has saved the home from the mortgage, has enabled business men to start again after their property was lost or their business swept away by panic, would read like a romance.

A life insurance policy has often made all the difference between home and no home, food and no food! It has saved multitudes of men from the humiliation of utter failure, and spared many families the shame of being turned out of their home.

Someone has said that it is not the high cost of living, but the cost of living high, that cripples so many lives and compels great ability to put up with the returns of mediocrity. Many people who are now poor, without homes, living from hand to mouth, have earned enough to have made them independent if they had used good sense in guarding their earnings.

I know of no other habit quite like that of the early formed habit of thrift; not the stingy, squeezing, holding-on habit, but the habit of wise living and spending, the wise administration of our money and our domestic affairs. A provident wife can establish such a system of household thrift that, combined with her husband's efforts, the family budget will take on remarkably large proportions and, within a short time, the possession of a home of their own may become an established fact.

In criticism of our American housewives it has been said over and over again that a French housewife would feed a family on what an average family throws away. Years ago, a great economist, Edward Atkinson, said that in the United States the waste from bad cooking alone was over a thousand million dollars a year. And our wastefulness and extravagance have gone on increasing in every direction.

The poor would be shocked if they were told that they were more extravagant than the well-to-do. Yet it is even so. The average poor woman in America, for instance, rarely knows how to buy food for the family economically. She does not, like the French woman, know how to buy the inexpensive cuts of meat and cook them so that they will be as palatable and nutritious as the more expensive ones. Nor does she know how to economize in other equally important details.

Since America entered the war, both our men of wealth and our housekeepers have been learning lessons in economy. Mr. Hoover and his army of assistants at the Food Department in Washington and all over this country are showing the necessity of economizing in every possible way, and instructing people in all ranks how to do it. Housewives are being taught food values and how to cook in the best and most economical way; inexpensive but nutritious menus are suggested, and thus women are shown how to make a good meal out of leftovers that formerly went into the garbage pail.

Women of all classes are especially cautioned in regard to the saving of food. They are asked to save every bit of meat, every crust of bread, stale or otherwise, even the crumbs; and not to pare potatoes, but to cook them with their jackets on. People are also advised to wear their old clothing as much as possible, instead of purchasing new, for we are told that our practice of economy will help win the war. Never before in the history of the world has the subject of economy and the necessity for thrift been so universally emphasized as to-day. Never before in this country has the word economy been so persistently dinned into our ears through the press, through posters, through the pulpit, through pamphlets, through lectures—in every possible way.

Are you learning that great lesson of the hour?

IX

"HE THAT SOWETH SPARINGLY SHALL REAP SPARINGLY"

MANY as are the maxims which urge the practice of economy, those which warn against false economy are almost equally numerous.

Solomon said: "There is that scattereth and yet increaseth; and there is that withholdeth more than is meet, but it tendeth to poverty." "Saving at the spigot and wasting at the bunghole," "Spoiling the ship to save a cent's worth of tar," and many another homely saying, reflect the common-sense view of forms of false economies which tend to loss instead of gain.

There are people who waste much more invaluable time in trying to save a little, by picayune methods, than the things saved are worth. I know a business man who makes his employees, as a matter of principle, save the string from packages, even if to save it takes twice as much time as the string is worth.

This man, also, in trying to save electricity, keeps his place of business so dark and dingy that he loses custom. He does not realize that a good light is the best kind of advertisement.

In trying to economize in petty ways thousands of men fail to do the bigger things possible for them. They develop a sort of mania for saving, for small economies, without realizing it, or how they are in danger of starving their minds and strangling their growth toward larger things.

You cannot afford to economize at the expense of mental strength, at the expense of efficiency. These are your stock in trade—the machinery and apparatus out of which you must carve your destiny. Do not tamper with your creative, productive ability. Keep up your standards at all hazards. This will enable you to produce to the maximum of your possibilities, for it keeps you in good health and in a condition to enjoy the largest, completest happiness.

Nothing surprises a young man more than the wonderful working of this law: "For whosoever hath, to him shall be given, and he shall have more abundance."

What a wonderful power there is in this law of increase. There is everything in holding the right view of economy, investing wisely, in keeping the mind upon plenty, carrying the abundance-thought instead of the limited, narrow, false economy thought.

"He that soweth sparingly shall reap sparingly" is just as true of the business man as of the farmer. Wise economy often means a very liberal expenditure.

I once knew a man who, in removing an old building to make way for a new one, left part of the old foundation, because he thought he thus could save several hundred dollars. The new building was several stories higher than the old one, but only a few weeks after it was completed it began to crack badly, and before any occupant moved in the whole structure collapsed. Everywhere in all lines of human endeavor we see the fatal effects of trying to save on foundations.

The youth in the past who pinched on his education, who did not think it worth while to prepare for very much of a career because he did not think he was going to be very much of a man; the youth who picked out the easy problems in school and skipped the hard ones, who slid along the lines of least resistance, who bragged that he got the best of his teacher in school by slighting his lessons, shirking, by cribbing in his examinations; the youth who was not willing to pay the price, not willing to sacrifice his desire for a good time in order to improve himself, has been heard from. He has been floundering along in his career, handicapped by his ignorance, held back by his lack of preparation. The great failure army is filled with human wrecks whose superstructure went down because of their superficial, faulty foundation.

I know a man who has always worked like a slave. He went into business for himself early in life, but has been under a perpetual handicap because in his youth he had thought it was foolish to waste so much time in laying an educational foundation and quit the grammar school before he was half through, and started out for himself. Because of his limited knowledge, his narrow, pinched foundation, he has always been placed at a great disadvantage with his competitors, who thought it worth while to be well informed and to lay broad, deep foundations. The result has been that his whole life has been marred, and he never has accomplished anything like what he might have accomplished but for this great lack. He never dreamed that the skipped problems way back in his boyhood, the neglected tasks, would reappear in his mature manhood, like Banquo's ghost, to mar both his success and his happiness. So during his later years this man has been trying to do very painfully and very imperfectly what he could have done so easily way back in his youth. The result of all this has been a limited career. The man has failed several times because he chose a career which was not in keeping with his lack of early training.

If he had not tried to save on his foundation, if he had been liberally prepared for the career which he chose, and had not had to spend such a large part of his life in trying to overcome his handicap, his lack, to strengthen his foundation after the superstructure was built, he would have had time to do the things which make for a broad, liberal manhood, and have become a man of some importance, a man who would have carried weight in his community. As it is, his life has been so starved and pinched that he has never passed for very much of a man.

How many parents in their eagerness to increase the family income deprive their children of a college or university education and rush them into business half prepared to meet opportunities for advancement that later come to them! They cannot send the boy or girl to school or college because "the rainy day" is a sort of specter which rises at every feast, whenever they try to get some enjoyment or satisfaction out of the present. They are always saving for some future time; always postponing things till next year, and this "next year" never comes.

How many of us economize in our friendships by neglecting them; economize in our social life, pleading with ourselves that we cannot afford to take the time for visiting and receiving visits! We economize on our vacations, until we are obliged to take long, enforced rests from the arduous duties of our business or profession, because the machinery of our bodies, so delicately and wonderfully made, has become so worn it is in danger of snapping at some vital point!

Many people live in such constant terror of "that terrible rainy day" that they do not enjoy the present. They deny themselves this and they cannot afford that; they postpone their real living; they just exist to-day, expecting really to live and enjoy themselves to-morrow. If they go away on a little vacation, or if they travel at all, they do it in a way which destroys most of the advantages they would otherwise get from it. They are afraid of spending a penny for anything but their actual fare and the barest necessaries.

I know of a New York business man who before the war traveled abroad and went to many interesting points, but he was too stingy to go into historic homes or buildings where any admission was charged. For example, he visited the homes of very famous characters, in different countries, homes which are regarded as shrines by thousands of intelligent people who have visited these countries, but he never entered them because he would not pay the price of admission. He said that he had seen the outside of the buildings, and that was enough. The result is that, though he has traveled considerably, he cannot talk interestingly, or even intelligently, about any place he has visited.

I have known people of means traveling abroad who were too stingy to buy Baedekers or other guide-books, and who would never think of hiring a guide to show them about, even in the most historic places. Does it not seem strange that people will spend so much money for traveling and then be too parsimonious to pay a little extra money to see the very things they had gone so far to see?

Sometimes liberality, which would seem to a smaller man extravagance, is the best kind of economy. Friendly help, inspiration, cultured acquaintances, are never too dearly bought at any price one can afford to pay. Everything must be measured by the end in view, the general result to be obtained.

It is not a question of whether a man can afford to pay ten or fifteen dollars for a seat at a banquet table considered by itself. He may pay fifteen dollars for his dinner, but he may get a hundred dollars' worth of inspiration from association with distinguished guests.

Such occasions are often a great stimulus to the ambition. They bring one in contact with persons of broader culture and wider experience, and it is wise expenditure to avail ourselves of everything within our reach which makes for culture and breadth of vision.

How much better it would be if you can possibly afford it to go where the leaders in your specialty lunch or dine, than to patronize a place where the atmosphere is not congenial to you! This opportunity for acquaintance and friendly relations with men of refinement would be worth very much more to you than the few cents or even the dollars you save by going to a cheaper place.

Of course, I would not advise anyone to commercialize his ability, or to try to sell his brains by wire-pulling methods, but I do advise those who are struggling to get on to form the acquaintance of those who can inspire and help them. It is a tremendous stimulus to one's ambition to come in close contact with thrifty, energetic people who are successful in one's own line of endeavor. We are more likely to do better ourselves, to bring out our full resources, when we associate with

JOHN D. ROCKEFELLER

them. To make the acquaintance of such people and know them is one of the most profitable investments a young person can make.

If one is after the largest, completest possible manhood, well-rounded, full-orbed, broad, then he will regard any expenditure to this end as the best kind of a paying investment, and he will not be held back by a false sense of economy or deceptive notions of extravagance.

Stuffing the pocketbook and starving the mind is pretty poor business, and is always an indication of a narrow outlook on life, a morbid view of things, a pinched mentality. The world is full of rich people who talk about leading the simple life when they mean the stingy life.

X

SPENDTHRIFTS OF TIME AND ENERGY

THE wise economist is the one who saves his time, who regards every moment as precious capital which he cannot afford to throw away, who regards his energy as a divine gift, too sacred to be foolishly expended.

The world is full of people who are plodding along in mediocrity who have enough ability to do something worth while if they would only get rid of the side issues, the non-essentials which eat up their time and sap their energy.

He who would make the most possible of his life must early learn to stop all leaks of power. The wasting of opportunities, time, and vital forces, constitutes the great tragedy of human life. It is the principal cause of unhappiness and failure. Many a man who is economical to stinginess in money matters, squanders with fearful prodigality his physical, mental, and moral energy and his time. He scorns a vacation, considering it a frightful waste of precious hours, loses needed sleep in working late at night at his desk, and is indifferent to regularity in eating. Such men pay the penalty in lowered vitality and a shortened business career.

Many busy people are shameful wasters of time and energy, simply because they do the lower things when higher ones are possible. They read a poor book when they might read a better one; they squander time with ordinary, purposeless companions when better ones are possible; they waste time in half-doing things, in botching, bungling and blundering, in doing things "just for now," doing things over and over, because they were not done right the first time.

I know a business man who is ambitious to do great things, but who gets so clogged up with details that he cannot seem to get out from under them. He tries to hurry with his work, but the little everlasting details constantly jump up and get away with such a large part of his time and energy that the day's work is always disappointing, and he leaves his office at night very unhappy. A confused mind is an ineffective mind.

The confused, excited mind is not only inefficient, but is likely to do some very foolish things. To guard against this, it is important to keep your mentality calm and balanced.

The next time things press you so hard on every hand that you do not know which way to turn, stop and take an inventory of the tasks to be done, and you will find that your confused mind, which is rapidly exhausting your vitality, is largely due to the fact that you are mentally trying to do many things at the same time. In other words, the sense of mental pressure is caused by the constant anticipation of the tasks ahead of you. Now, when you know you can only attend to one thing at a time, why not shut out everything else until you are through with that one, and then take the next, and so on to the end, without attempting to do these things over and over again by anticipation?

If we could only learn thus to concentrate the mind intensely upon the things we are doing and shut out everything else until its turn came, we would never have that sense of confusion and pressure which so interferes with efficiency and happiness.

There was in process of building, in England, a clock in an edifice in which many lawyers had their offices, and there was often a large congregation of them in the lobby and corridors.

The clockmaker sent one of his men for a motto to put under the mammoth clock. The messenger asked the first man he met, who, not knowing what the boy meant, said: "Begone about your business!"

The clockmaker received the motto, as the messenger delivered it, with surprise; but after thinking a moment, decided to use it. It served as a quiet reminder to loungers, as it ticked off the minutes that were as fleeting as the sun's rays.

The men who accomplish things, who do big things in a big way, protect their executive ability by all sorts of safeguards. Many men keep secretaries as a sort of buffer to protect themselves from people who steal their time.

We may not begrudge our time to people who have claims upon us, or who give us some compensating advantage, or to those who need our assistance; but it is exasperating to be obliged to sit for half an hour or an hour and listen to some irrelevant matter which does not interest us, just because we do not want to appear rude.

It is not alone in the busy office that we find these spendthrifts of time and energy; they are just as frequently seen in our homes. The housewife, while in the midst of her domestic duties, is called to the telephone to listen to a garrulous neighbor's latest gossip, or in response to the door-bell a friendly visitor appears with long-drawn-out tale of domestic tribulations.

Some women are always dropping in to chat with the busy woman who is trying her best to get a little time for the things worth while. These idle, purposeless women sit and chat and chat until the opportunity for doing what the ambitious, energetic woman longed to do has gone by. If such people only realized the preciousness of time, the great value of a single day, they would not let it slip through their fingers so lightly or treat it so flippantly.

"There can be no thrift or ultimate success where hour is not fastened to hour and moment woven into moment in the great pattern of life," says a writer on "Life's Waste."

"The waste of time is life's greatest blunder and most destructive force. In the fragments is an abundance of opportunity. Oh, how ruinous waste has shattered the hopes and ambitions of men! It has been the author of despair and even death to the best in life. The greatest discovery of young life is the value of time. . . . The value which a man places upon the moments of to-day is the author of all good in every to-morrow."

Think of the possibilities that live in a single day! Think of what it would mean to someone, somewhere,—to the producer of great masterpieces in art and science!

When you start out in the morning just try to picture to yourself the wonderful value of that day. Just think what you would make of it if you knew you would never have another—what every minute would mean to you! How you would crowd values into it! Every second would be precious.

"There are moments," says Dean Alford, "which are worth more than years. We cannot help it. There is no proportion between spaces of time in importance or in value. A stray, unthought-of five minutes may contain the event of a life. And this all-important moment—who can tell when it will be upon us?"

Every day is a precious gift from the Creator—fresh, beautiful, filled with magnificent possibilities. Don't squander it in useless motions and wasted energies; don't idle it away; don't watch the clock and wish it away. Don't throw it away; don't waste it; don't kill it; for your future lives in it.

XI

THE BANK-BOOK HABIT

"Sow an Act and you reap a Habit,
Sow a Habit and you reap a Character,
Sow a Character and you reap a Destiny."

WHEN the Board of Education of New York City decided to run penny banks in the public schools to encourage the pupils in thrift, Vice-President Greene said: "The Board of Education wants to make the pupils thrifty as well as wise. It wants to remove inducements to extravagance and to encourage them to take care of their pennies until their savings have reached an amount that will enable them to open individual accounts with the banks. At present their few pennies do not enable them to do this."

Thus thousands of young people were given an opportunity, and were encouraged to form the bank-book habit, which has since enabled many of them to invest in Liberty Bonds, and in this way they are helping their country as well as themselves.

We must not overlook the physical basis of

habit. It is very difficult to do things we have not formed a habit of doing. The nerves controlling the muscles are dependent upon the brain and respond to its reactions, learn its habits, and do automatically whatever the brain has formed a habit of doing.

If we have formed careless, spendthrift habits, habits which drag us in the opposite direction from that we wish to go, we must put out an enormous amount of energy to fight against their grip; for habit is second nature and gets as strong a hold upon us as our original temperamental tendencies. We are placed at the tremendous disadvantage of trying to form new tracks for thought, new highways for habit, at the same time that we are trying to obliterate the deep furrows which a thousand repetitions have already made in the brain and nerve centers.

For all practical purposes, habit for a middle-aged person is fate, it is almost hopelessly certain that what has been done every day for twenty years will be repeated thereafter. We imagine that we can break a bad habit at any time, but it usually takes just about twice as long to break a habit as it did to make it.

When Rip Van Winkle said "I won't count this time," he gave voice to a very common delusion. But though it was easy for him to say that he would not "count" this lapse or that into his old habit, the cells of the brain "counted" it; as Prof. James said, every nerve and fiber in his organism were counting it. Down deep in his nervous centers there was a call for alcoholic stimulant so loud, so insistent that Rip Van Winkle was practically powerless to resist it. Every cent he had and some that he did not have went for drink. It is the same with the spendthrift habit. It is one of the hardest to break and one of the most ruinous to fall into. On the other hand, the bank-book habit is one of the best friends a boy or girl, a young man or young woman, can make.

Every child should be started in life with a bank account, however small, and something should be constantly added to this sum, no matter how little, if for no other reason than to implant in his mind the idea of saving, and the larger idea of thrift. A child should grow up with the idea that it is absolutely necessary to his self-respect, his safety, to have a little money between himself and want, something which will stand as a protection, a buffer, between himself and the demanding world in case of necessity.

"There is a real exhilaration in a bank account, even if it is not a large one," says the Rev. Dr. C. H. Parkhurst. "A young fellow recently had a certain amount, not a large sum, put to his credit in a savings bank. It made an epoch in his history, and when six months later his passbook was written up and showed an interest accumulation of five dollars and twenty-two cents it straightened him up to three inches above the ordinary height, and he declared that he felt as though he belonged to the capitalistic class and was moving among the high moneyed circles."

The moment a young man begins to save systematically and appreciates the true value of money he necessarily becomes a larger man. He takes broader views of life. He begins to have a better opinion of himself. Trust takes the place of doubt, his savings are the actual demonstration that he has not only the ability to earn, but also to keep his money, and, as has been said before, it takes greater wisdom to hold on to money than to make it.

Thousands of men have blessed the day that they opened a savings-bank account with the resolution to deposit regularly, for it brought a new motive into their lives. It developed in them the habit of thrift. It taught them many a lesson of improved business methods, improved judgment, because of enforced thrift and economy, which are so dependent upon system and order.

The knowledge that he has been able to save has given many a youth more confidence in himself. It has made him a better employee, and he will undertake greater responsibilities because of it.

All this means that his earning power is largely increased.

It is the "man with the savings-bank habit who seldom gets laid off; he's the one who can get along without you, but you cannot get along without him."

Nothing makes a business man so absolutely independent as ready cash.

The very reputation of always having a good bank balance shows a clear head, good business judgment. It is a great thing to make your signature stand for something—never to have your credit questioned—to have everybody say you are good pay and quick pay.

A schoolboy who was asked to state the greatest event of the year said that it was the fact that he had saved fifty dollars. From one point of view, he was not so wide of the mark. The first fifty dollars he saves is really one of the most important things in one's life.

There is an infinite meaning in little savings. They are the germs of a greater fortune. Many people would be surprised at the vast accumulations made in a lifetime by the continual and persistent saving of petty accounts which they despised. The tendency of money judiciously invested is to multiply—the more you get the faster it accumulates, just like the small boy's snowball, the more he rolls it in the snow, the larger it grows.

A few hundred dollars or a thousand in a savings bank has often made all the difference between success and failure. I know of a concern which has estimated assets of one hundred and fifty thousand dollars, yet it was forced to the wall for the lack of five thousand dollars ready cash.

A bank of any standing must have a surplus. Every young man of standing should have a surplus of savings, no matter how small. Start it. Keep adding to it.

The youth who is careless of his change, who thinks that a nickel or a dime or a quarter has very little to do with a fortune, is forming a habit that may cripple him for life.

Most people, especially young people, do not appreciate the value of small savings. They think that if they had a large amount it would pay to put it in the bank, or to make this or that investment, but that they could not do much with a small amount. The result is they keep their small savings about them, and this is a constant temptation to spend, for there are always scores of ways of getting rid of loose change. It is very slippery.

I was quite impressed recently by a remark of a young man, who said that he had been carrying his money loosely in his pocket for several years, and he had found that it slipped away so fast, for all sorts of things which he might have gotten along without, that he tried the experiment of carrying all his money in a purse. The result is that he finds it much easier to save, because he says he has time to think before he gets his money out of his purse, and he often decides not to buy what he would have bought had his change been so handy that he could put his hand on it in an instant.

The saving habit is a character builder, because if we are willing to make the sacrifice or to practice the self-control, to forego the passing pleasures for something more permanent, we are making it more and more certain that we shall not throw away on foolish, frivolous things these savings, which have cost us so much.